NICK FAWCETT

A Chequered LEGACY

The Good, the Bad and the Ugly of the Church

Book 1: An Advent Course
The Good

www.kevinmayhew.com

KM PUBLISHING

First published in Great Britain in 2014 by Kevin Mayhew Ltd
Buxhall, Stowmarket, Suffolk IP14 3BW
Tel: +44 (0) 1449 737978 Fax: +44 (0) 1449 737834
E-mail: info@kevinmayhew.com

www.kevinmayhew.com

9 8 7 6 5 4 3 2 1 0

ISBN 978 1 84867 729 6
Catalogue No. 1501451

Cover design by Rob Mortonson
© Images used under licence from Shutterstock Inc.
Typeset by Richard Weaver

Printed and bound in Great Britain

Contents

About the author

Brought up in Southend-in-Sea, Essex, Nick Fawcett trained for the Baptist ministry at Bristol and Oxford, before serving churches in Lancashire and Cheltenham. He subsequently spent three years as a chaplain with the Christian movement Toc H, before focusing on writing and editing, which he continues with today, despite wrestling with myeloma, a currently incurable cancer of the bone marrow. He lives with his wife, Deborah, and two children – Samuel and Kate – in Wellington, Somerset, worshipping, when able, at the local Anglican church. A keen walker, he delights in the beauty of the Somerset and Devon countryside around his home, his numerous books owing much to the inspiration he unfailingly finds there.

Introduction

What is the greatest enemy of the Christian faith? Strange as it may seem, the answer could, with some justification, be put forward as the Church. Such a suggestion sounds ludicrous, doesn't it – a contradiction in terms! And so, to a point, it *is*, for beyond doubt the Church is also the greatest friend that the Christian faith will ever have. Yet, as many a militant atheist, or even sceptical agnostic, will quickly point out, the Church's history is hardly one to be proud of, littered as it is with all kinds of errors, aberrations, even crimes that make a mockery of everything Jesus taught and that Christians are meant to stand for. The Spanish Inquisition, burning of witches, wars in the name of religion, persecution of other Christians or those of other faiths, and, more recently, rampant sexism and homophobia, not to mention child abuse scandals, have repeatedly dragged the Church's name through the mud; truly a legacy to be ashamed of. Sadly, yet seemingly almost inevitably, organised religion by definition runs the risk of destroying the very thing it sets out to embody and safeguard. The kernel of truth that gives it birth becomes lost under a husk of accretions, as well-meaning (and not-so-well-meaning) believers seek to prescribe just what that truth is. Each defines God in their own image and, usually, according to their own interests.

Yet, as I've said, such a negative and bleak assessment does not give the complete picture. In all kinds of ways the Church has been a force for good across the centuries, seeking to make known the love of Christ in word and deed, striving in ways large and small to help build a better world. I've been privileged personally to know a host of wonderful Christians who throughout their lives have attempted to translate faith into action, their example offering untold inspiration and enrichment. And a significant percentage of voluntary caring work within this country is still undertaken by Christian believers and organisations, seeking to ameliorate the lot of others, to the extent that if their services were to be withdrawn, the consequences for many, and for society at large, would be devastating. For all its unquestionable faults, the Church also has numerous virtues to learn from and build upon.

In this two-volume study book I want to explore what – to steal the title of the classic spaghetti western – we might term the good, the bad and the ugly of the Church. Starting in Advent, we look at the positive, celebrating some of the achievements of Christian believers across the years in terms of building a better world, and asking what their efforts and example might teach us today. In the Lent book, we will move on to faults of the Church; faults that call us to reflect, confess, repent and work as best we can for a better, more enlightened future. Let me urge you to treat both books as a pair, and not to follow one without moving on to the other. To do the latter would risk giving you a completely false picture, either reinforcing a misplaced sense of complacency or leading to an overly jaundiced appraisal of the Church, past, present and future. We have a chequered history, there's no getting away from it: a mixture of the inspiring and appalling, wonderful and awful, and we need to learn from both. Through doing so honestly, we may perhaps open the way for God to help us become more fully the people he would have us be.

Nick Fawcett

A voice for freedom – William Wilberforce

Opening prayer

Lord Jesus Christ,
you came into our world
and lived and died among us
in order to set us free from everything that holds us captive.
Thank you for that glorious freedom,
and thank you for those who, in turn,
work – or laboured in times past –
to bring freedom for others from whatever denies, destroys or
negates life.
Especially we thank you for those who, in your name,
strove to overcome and outlaw the evil of slavery,
determined that all should enjoy the liberty and dignity
they deserve.
Help us to learn from the mistakes of the past
and to build on the achievements,
so that we, in some small way,
may contribute to building a better world
and to bringing nearer the dawn of your kingdom.
Amen.

Key passage

When he came to Nazareth, where he had been brought up, he
went to the synagogue on the sabbath day, as was his custom. He
stood up to read, and the scroll of the prophet Isaiah was given to
him. He unrolled the scroll and found the place where it was
written: 'The Spirit of the Lord is upon me, because he has
anointed me to bring good news to the poor. He has sent me to
proclaim release to the captives and recovery of sight to the blind,
to let the oppressed go free, to proclaim the year of the Lord's favour.'

Luke 4:16-19

Context.
Beginning of ministry to Israel
Citing Is. 61:1-2   Good News of Deliverance 7
to a faithless people

[left margin: Put response upon Jesus + object]

[handwritten: i) of Gospel (prospects), ii) of passage, iii) of social, moral, polit of day]

[handwritten: As real Script ... need context]

Introduction

'To set the oppressed free' – such was seen by Jesus as an integral part of his ministry and such has been viewed since by generations of Christians as an essential aspect of their calling, too. Advent, perhaps more than any other time, challenges us to reflect on that mission, for it speaks not only of the one who came in fulfilment of God's promises of old, but also of our responsibility, in turn, to work for a better world and brighter future in his name. So how well have Christians honoured that calling?

We focus in this session on one issue in particular on which the Church has a chequered legacy but in which a celebrated individual – William Wilberforce – worked tirelessly to set the oppressed free: namely, that of slavery. Living, as we do in the twenty-first century, it's hard to believe that anyone, let alone Christians, could ever have sanctioned something as patently iniquitous as the slave trade, yet sanction it many did. Thankfully, the voices of faith lifted up against it finally overcame those raised in support. What can we learn from the story of that confrontation in terms of life and faith today? *[handwritten: How we use Scripture]*

Draughts activity

See the Appendix.

[handwritten: → What is the single unique thing that ... made slavery so a shame]

Study

Sometime during the middle of the fifteenth century, the crew of a Portuguese sailing ship moored alongside the west coast of Africa set about capturing native inhabitants, carrying them off and selling them back in Europe as slaves. It was the start of a vile commercial system that was to blight the world for nearly three hundred years, and that was to see traders from Spain, Portugal, the Netherlands, Britain and, eventually, America involved in the enslavement of anything up to 11 million West Africans, barbarically plucked from their home country and set to work in conditions that led to the premature death of many and appalling suffering for most. Films and TV series like *Roots* and *Twelve Years*

[handwritten margin: 3) How relevant today i) social ii) individual]

a Slave have graphically brought home, should any reminder be needed, just how evil the trade was, and how awful its impact.

Not, though, that slavery was anything new. It had been around already for thousands of years, dating back to the days of the early Greek empire and beyond. Nor has the record of the Church been anything like exemplary over the years. Many passages in the Bible can be seen as condoning, or at least accepting, slavery, Colossians 3:22 and Ephesians 6:5, for example, calling for slaves to obey their masters, and 1 Peter 2:18 urging, 'Slaves, in reverent fear of God submit yourselves to your masters, not only to those who are good and considerate, but also to those who are harsh.' Christians captured Muslims throughout the Crusades and sold them into slavery, just as Muslims had done to them. The Catholic Church supported the Portuguese slave trade and in 1710 the plantation owner, Christopher Codrington, left his 800-acre Barbados estate – the working and wealth of which was entirely dependent on slaves – to the Anglican Church's newly established Society for the Propagation of the Christian Religion in Foreign Parts (SPG). Much of the Church of England's subsequent wealth, and indeed that of other denominations, sprang directly from the slave trade. Certain bishops in Britain even owned slaves, and generally the attitude among Christians was that Africans were unenlightened heathens and less than fully human, for whom slavery was thus perfectly acceptable.

Yet if the Church can by no means be exempt from criticism, it nonetheless deserves praise for the role of many in its ranks in eventually bringing slavery to an end. Among the first of those to oppose it were nonconformists – Quakers, Presbyterians, Methodists, Congregationalists and Baptists – perhaps because these had first-hand experience of what it meant to be abused and persecuted. Quakers, in particular, emphasised that everyone is equal in the sight of God, and in 1696 it officially declared its opposition to the slave trade. A book written in 1772 by the Quaker writer Anthony Benezet, titled *Some Historical Account of Guinea*, was followed in 1774 by John Wesley's *Thoughts upon Slavery*, both of which helped to fuel growing calls for abolition. The latter, though, would not be easily achieved. Vested interests – including among Christians of all persuasions – would not relinquish their source of wealth lightly. It would take one man in particular, and a long, challenging campaign in the face of bitter opposition, to help finally to end this terrible wrong.

William Wilberforce – a voice for freedom

'So enormous, so dreadful, so irremediable did the Trade's wickedness appear that my own mind was completely made up for Abolition. Let the consequences be what they would, I from this time determined that I would never rest until I had effected its abolition.' So declared the great English politician, philanthropist and reformer, William Wilberforce, in his celebrated abolition speech to the House of Commons on 12 May 1789. It was the start of a 44-year-long campaign that would finally see not just the slave trade abolished in the British colonies, but, just three days before his death, the official abolition of slavery itself.

Born into a wealthy merchant family in Hull in 1759, William enjoyed the extravagant distractions of fashionable society during his formative years, graduated from St John's, Cambridge, in 1781, and was elected an MP in 1780, aged just 21. Between 1884 and 1886 he was converted to evangelical Christianity and for a time he toyed with leaving parliament, but friends – including the celebrated hymn writer John Newton, a one-time slave trader turned pastor – urged him that he could serve God more effectively from a position of influence within public life. Putting an end to the slave trade soon became William's passion, after he talked first with Sir Charles Middleton, who urged him to take up the cause in parliament, and then with Thomas Clarkson, campaigner and writer of *An Essay on the Slavery and Commerce of the Human Species*, who was to become a friend and ally for the next half-century and more.

If Wilberforce had hoped for a warm response to his campaign he was to be swiftly disillusioned, for he was to meet instead with fierce and bitter hostility. His opponents used every means at their disposal to frustrate his attempts at introducing legislation, on one occasion, for example, handing out free opera tickets to various abolition supporters on the evening of a crucial vote. Two attempts were even made on his life by slave-ship captains, who feared an end to their lucrative trade. Yet despite threats to his safety and a growing toll on his health – it is thought that he suffered from ulcerative colitis for many years of his life – William stayed firm, encouraged by friends such as John Wesley, who told him, 'If God is with you, who can be against you? . . . Be not weary in well-doing. Go on . . . till even American slavery, the vilest that ever saw the sun, shall vanish away.' His speeches and writings blazed with passion, such as in the following: '. . . if the slave trade be a national crime, declared by every wise and respectable man of all parties, without exception, to be a compound of the grossest wickedness and cruelty, a crime to which we cling in defiance of the clearest light, not only in opposition to our own acknowledgements of its guilt but even of our own declared resolutions to abandon it; is not this then a time in which all who are not perfectly sure that the Providence of God is but a fable, should be strenuous in their endeavours to lighten the vessel of the state, of such a load of guilt and infamy?'

Eventually, in the year those words were published (1807), Wilberforce met with success, parliament resounding to the sound of cheering as the slave trade abolition bill was passed. Not that this meant the end of the battle. Slavery was to continue in many parts of the British Empire for a further sixteen years, and William was to continue to campaign and fight tirelessly against it, despite his health declining so badly that, in 1926, he felt constrained to resign his seat in parliament. Finally, in 1833, the practice of slavery was abolished throughout the empire – just a month after Wilberforce delivered his final abolitionist speech (at a rally in Maidstone, Kent) and a mere few days before his death. His achievements are well summed up by the inscription on the statue of him erected in his honour in Westminster Abbey: 'To the memory of William Wilberforce . . . who . . . by the blessing of God, removed from England the guilt of the African slave trade, and prepared the way for the abolition of slavery in every colony of the Empire. In the prosecution of these objects he relied, not in vain, on God; but in the progress he was called to endure great obloquy and great opposition.'

Old Testament verses

[handwritten: Is Many, varied, as wd expect. Not Book, library →]

So what does the Bible have to say about slavery? The answer may surprise and disturb you, for, as noted earlier, its message is ambivalent. If anything, Scripture seems to take slavery as a given and to advocate tacit or outright acceptance of the practice. Here are the key Old Testament passages:

[handwritten: Follows from 20 - Ten Comm..ts]

Exodus 21:2-11

[handwritten: Ironic: release from Egypt. Whole Exodus narrative is. Yet Hebrew slave - even Canaanites more so]

When you buy a male Hebrew slave, he shall serve for six years, but in the seventh he shall go out a free person, without debt. If he comes in single, he shall go out single; if he comes in married, then his wife shall go out with him. If his master gives him a wife and she bears him sons or daughters, the wife and her children shall be her master's and he shall go out alone. But if the slave declares, 'I love my master, my wife, and my children; I will not go out a free person', then his master shall bring him before God. He shall be brought to the door or the doorpost; and his master shall pierce his ear with an awl; and he shall serve him for life.

When a man sells his daughter as a slave, she shall not go out as the male slaves do. If she does not please her master, who designated her for himself, then he shall let her be redeemed; he shall have no right to sell her to a foreign people, since he has dealt unfairly with her. If he designates her for his son, he shall deal with her as with a daughter. If he takes another wife to himself, he shall not diminish the food, clothing, or marital rights of the first wife. And if he does not do these three things for her, she shall go out without debt, without payment of money.

Exodus 21:20, 21

When a slave-owner strikes a male or female slave with a rod and the slave dies immediately, the owner shall be punished. But if the slave survives for a day or two, there is no punishment; for the slave is the owner's property.

Exodus 21:26, 27

When a slave-owner strikes the eye of a male or female slave, destroying it, the owner shall let the slave go, a free person, to compensate for the eye. If the owner knocks out a tooth of a male or female slave, the slave shall be let go, a free person, to compensate for the tooth.

Leviticus 19:20

If a man has sexual relations with a woman who is a slave, designated for another man but not ransomed or given her freedom, an inquiry shall be held. They shall not be put to death, since she has not been freed.

Leviticus 25:39

If any who are dependent on you become so impoverished that they sell themselves to you, you shall not make them serve as slaves.

Leviticus 25:44-46

As for the male and female slaves whom you may have, it is from the nations around you that you may acquire male and female slaves. You may also acquire them from among the aliens residing with you, and from their families that are with you, who have been born in your land; and they may be your property. You may keep them as a possession for your children after you, for them to inherit as property. These you may treat as slaves, but as for your fellow Israelites, no one shall rule over the other with harshness.

Deuteronomy 23:15, 16

Slaves who have escaped to you from their owners shall not be given back to them. They shall reside with you, in your midst, in any place they choose in any one of your towns, wherever they please; you shall not oppress them.

Discussion

What do you make of those passages? They're a mixed bag, aren't they! Look at them again and spend some time discussing together what each one is saying, and how, if at all, it is possible to reconcile them to our abhorrence of slavery today in any shape or form? Can a simplistic understanding of the Bible as the literal and inerrant word of God stand up to scrutiny? Are there any positive aspects in the Old Testament's understanding of and attitude towards slavery?

New Testament verses

Let's look now at some New Testament passages:

[handwritten: Parts of wider reflection on other + household roles — hust | wife; parent | child; Master | slave]

Ephesians 6:5

[handwritten circle: 5:22 – 6:9]

Slaves, obey your earthly masters with fear and trembling, in singleness of heart, as you obey Christ.

Galatians 3:28

There is no longer Jew or Greek, there is no longer slave or free, there is no longer male and female; for all of you are one in Christ Jesus.

[handwritten: Rules for Christian household]

Colossians 3:22

[handwritten circle: 3:18 – 4:1 Part of longer reflection on order]

Slaves, obey your earthly masters in everything, not only while being watched and in order to please them, but wholeheartedly, fearing the Lord.

[handwritten: NB Masters treat slaves justly knowing you also have a Master in Heaven]

Colossians 4:1

Masters, treat your slaves justly and fairly, for you know that you also have a Master in heaven.

1 Timothy 6:1, 2

Let all who are under the yoke of slavery regard their masters as worthy of all honour, so that the name of God and the teaching may not be blasphemed. Those who have believing masters must not be disrespectful to them on the ground that they are members of the church; rather they must serve them all the more, since those who benefit by their service are believers and beloved.

Titus 2:9, 10   2:1-10   *Cmds ct of older men, women*
younger men

Tell slaves to be submissive to their masters and to give satisfaction in every respect; they are not to answer back, not to pilfer, but to show complete and perfect fidelity, so that in everything they may be an ornament to the doctrine of God our Saviour.

NB 2:11 – Salvation to all
–15

Philemon 1:10, 12-16

I am appealing to you for my child, Onesimus, whose father I have become during my imprisonment. I am sending him, that is, my own heart, back to you. I wanted to keep him with me, so that he might be of service to me in your place during my imprisonment for the gospel; but I preferred to do nothing without your consent, in order that your good deed might be voluntary and not something forced. Perhaps this is the reason he was separated from you for a while, so that you might have him back for ever, no longer as a slave but as more than a slave, a beloved brother – especially to me but how much more to you, both in the flesh and in the Lord.

Model of Christ's
suffering
+ obedience

1 Peter 2:18   1 Pete 2:18 – 3:7

Slaves, accept the authority of your masters with all deference, not only those who are kind and gentle but also those who are harsh.

Discussion

- How do these verses compare with the Old Testament ones?
- Do you find them ambiguous on the matter of slavery?
- Are they any easier to reconcile with our modern-day perspective?
- What do you make of the story of Philemon and Onesimus? Is Paul making a general case against slavery here?
- What positive principles are encouraged in these verses? Are these in any way sufficient to outweigh the apparent acceptance of slavery?

- Many Christians, including clergy, attempted to justify slavery by arguing that Scripture speaks of being simultaneously a good slave and a Christian, and even that it is a good thing to suffer as a slave; see 1 Peter 2:18-25). How does that make you feel? How does it shape you attitude towards the Bible?
- What verses could opponents of slavery have used to support their case? What biblical principles could be used to refute the practice?

Quotes

Reflect individually on the following quotations for a moment, then discuss together which, if any, people found most helpful, and why. What point is each making? What lessons can be learned from them? What challenge do they make to us, personally, and to the Church in general.

- You may choose to look the other way but you can never say again that you did not know. (William Wilberforce) Universal - Nazi - child abuse
- If to be feelingly alive to the sufferings of my fellow-creatures is to be a fanatic, I am one of the most incurable fanatics ever permitted to be at large. (William Wilberforce)
- Those who deny freedom to others deserve it not for themselves, and, under a just God, cannot retain it. (Abraham Lincoln)
- Whenever I hear anyone arguing for slavery, I feel a strong impulse to see it tried on him personally. (Abraham Lincoln)
- As I would not be a slave, so I would not be a master. This expresses my idea of democracy. (Abraham Lincoln)
- Slaves sing most when they are most unhappy. The songs of the slave represent the sorrows of his heart; and he is relieved by them, only as an aching heart is relieved by its tears. (Frederick Douglass)

Final thoughts

In 2006, the General Synod of the Church of England passed a motion acknowledging and apologising for the 'dehumanising and shameful' consequences of slavery. Its representatives, like

Christians the world over, were – and remain – all too aware of the chequered legacy of the Church. At least Christians can claim to have been at the forefront of the campaign against one of the greatest evils that blighted out world. We should celebrate that, not with any sense of smugness and self-righteousness, but through committing ourselves in turn to working for a better world – a world in which, tragically, slavery is not only still a reality but a growing problem, up to 30 million people estimated to be enduring a form of slavery today. Take time to learn more about the issue, and reflect on what response you can make to it.

Closing prayer

Hear our prayer, Lord, for those denied their freedom –
those who are forced to work without pay,
subjected to threats and violence,
sold for sex,
trafficked as objects,
tortured, abused, exploited, oppressed:
a host of people for whom slavery is not some abstract memory
but a horrific daily reality.
Support and strengthen all organisations, protest groups
and campaigners
who work to bring this evil to the attention of nations
and governments,
and stir the hearts of people everywhere to do all in their power
to bring it to an end.
Grant release to the captives,
this and every day.
Amen.

Common Good

Jim Wallis 3,5,8

GS 6 ;8,10 ,26

Rowan Williams p2 *

cf debate at GS on bedroom tax - amendment that
Church institutions invest in social housing - Church Commissioners
+ Pension fund reps pleaded duty to maximise return

A voice for justice – The Earl of Shaftesbury

Opening prayer

Loving God,
you call us to seek justice,
not just for ourselves but for all.
You urge us to be compassionate in our dealings with others,
to put their interests before our own,
to care for the poor, the weak and the needy,
and to do what we can in making this world a fairer place for all.
Speak today through the example of those who have done just that,
and inspire us, in turn, to respond to you and to others
more faithfully,
reaching out in the name of Christ, through word and deed,
to minister something of your love.
Help us to build on what has been good in the history of
your people,
and to move away from what has been bad,
so that we may contribute towards a more fitting and lasting legacy,
that truly redounds to your glory.
Amen.

Key passages

Take away from me the noise of your songs; I will not listen to the
melody of your harps. But let justice roll down like waters, and
righteousness like an ever-flowing stream.

Amos 5:23, 24

He has told you, O mortal, what is good; and what does the Lord
require of you but to do justice, and to love kindness, and to walk
humbly with your God?

Micah 6:8

Introduction

The words above, of two of the so-called minor prophets, eloquently capture a theme that runs throughout Scripture: that of our responsibility to pursue justice whenever and wherever we can. It is a calling that the Church has a highly mixed record in discharging. While Christians have sometimes stood at the forefront of campaigns for social reform, as often as not in times past they have equally supported the status quo even when this has been patently oppressive and unjust. Indeed, as we will be touching upon during this session, many of the mill and factory owners who imposed draconian working conditions upon their employees - including women and children – were frequently respected nonconformist figures within their community, many justifying the Protestant work ethic upon Scripture. Thankfully, others – in particular, Lord Shaftesbury – believed that compassionate care of workers, and of the poor and disadvantaged in general, was an integral aspect of Christian discipleship, not an optional extra but fundamental to our faith. Their message and example still need to be recognised and reflected on today.

Draughts activity

See the Appendix.

Study

Two children I know got employment in a factory when they were five years old . . . the spinning men or women employ children if they can get a child to do their business . . . the child is paid one shilling or one shilling and six pence, and they will take that child before they take an older one who will cost more.

(George Gould, a Manchester merchant, 1816)

The smallest children in the factories were scavengers . . . they go under the machine, while it is going . . . it is very dangerous when they first come, but they become used to it.

(Charles Aberdeen, a Manchester cotton factory worker, 1832)

We went to the mill at five in the morning. We worked until dinner time and then to nine or ten at night; on Saturday it could be till eleven and often till twelve at night. We were sent to clean the machinery on the Sunday.

(A former child mill worker, interviewed in 1849)

I began work at the mill in Bradford when I was nine years old . . . we began at six in the morning and worked until nine at night. When business was brisk, we began at five and worked until ten in the evening.

(Hannah Brown, interviewed in 1832)

Woodward and other overlookers used to beat me with pieces of thick leather straps made supple by oil, and having an iron buckle at the end, drew blood almost every time it was applied.

(John Brown, quoted in the *Lion* newspaper in 1828)

Sarah Golding was poorly and so she stopped her machine. James Birch, the overlooker, knocked her to the floor. She got up as well as she could. He knocked her down again. Then she was carried to her house . . . she was found dead in her bed. There was another girl called Mary . . . she knocked her food can to the floor. The master, Mr Newton, kicked her and caused her to wear away till she died. There was another, Caroline Thompson, who was beaten till she went out of her mind. The overlookers used to cut off the hair of any girl caught talking to a lad. This head shaving was a dreadful punishment. We were more afraid of it than any other punishment, for girls are proud of their hair.

(Former child cotton mill worker, interviewed in 1849)

I have seen my master, Luke Taylor, with a horse whip standing outside the mill when the children have come too late . . . he lashed them all the way to the mill.

(John Fairbrother, an overlooker, interviewed in 1819)

Recollections such as the above give us just a tiny flavour of the appalling conditions experienced by child workers in mid-Victorian Britain. It was a time of plenty for many – above all for the new breed of entrepreneurs and nouveau riche, as well as the emerging middle classes – but for those at the bottom of the pile – manual workers, the unemployed, debtors, children and orphans – life was frequently a grinding struggle, little different from slavery. Their working hours, as we have seen, were long; conditions were dangerous; discipline was strict if not brutal; and wages were poor: the average wage in the 1850s was about fifteen shillings (75p) a week. Many children got just five shillings (25p) or considerably less, such as the one shilling (5p) cited above. Such pay and conditions were justified by many industrialists of the grounds of religion – the so-called Protestant work ethic, in particular, maintaining that hard work should be undertaken not for earthly but for heavenly reward. It was also taught that God had instituted the social order, giving each person their place within it, and that it was not for people to question his mysterious ways. Hence, the notorious third verse of the hymn 'All things bright and beautiful', written by Mrs Cecil Alexander and first published in 1848:

> The rich man in his castle,
> the poor man at his gate,
> God made them high and lowly,
> and ordered their estate.

Some of the worse jobs children were involved in have been well documented. Many, for example, were employed as chimney sweeps, sent scrambling up chimneys when aged just five or six. Should they get stuck in the chimney, as they often did, a common practice was for the Master Chimney Sweeper simply to light the fire below, forcing the child to extricate themselves or die of suffocation. Countless children worked in mills and factories, as recorded above, these being not only cheaper to employ but also small enough to crawl into places adults couldn't reach – and should they be injured or killed during the course of their work, as frequently happened, then there were plenty of other waifs and strays on hand at the nearest orphanage. Typically their job was to clean machines while they were still running, many as a result losing fingers or limbs, or even being crushed to death. Numerous other children lived rough on the streets, polishing shoes, running errands, or selling matches, firewood, buttons, flowers, bootlaces or the like in a desperate attempt to make a living. Others, again, worked in the coal mines, often in dark and dangerous shafts for up to twelve hours a day. Some, called 'drawers', were chained to heavy carts of coal which they had to haul up to the surface. 'I sit in the dark down in the pit for twelve hours a day,' wrote one seven-year-old boy. 'I only see daylight on Sundays when I don't work down the pit. Once, I fell asleep and a wagon ran over my leg.' A ten-year-old girl's memories are equally shocking: 'I have a belt round my waist, and a chain passing between my legs, and I go on my hands and feet. The tunnels are narrow and very wet where I work. My clothes are wet through almost all day long.'

It was in response to appalling abuses such as these that Anthony Ashley-Cooper, 7th Earl of Shaftesbury, began a lifetime of campaigning for social justice that was to transform the lives of hundreds of thousands of people.

Anthony Ashley-Cooper, 7th Earl of Shaftesbury – a voice for justice

Despite being the eldest son of the 6th Earl of Shaftesbury (1768–1851) and Lady Anne Spencer-Churchill (1773–1865), Ashley – as he was known – knew first-hand what it was to suffer abuse and neglect, albeit that in his case it had come at the hands of his father, and the teachers at his boarding school. His childhood, we are told, was a deeply unhappy one, leaving him prone to bouts of depression for the rest of his life.

Elected MP for Woodstock – a conservative seat controlled by his uncle, the Duke of Marlborough – and, later, Dorchester, his early parliamentary career seemed unpromising. An interest in social issues, however, was kindled by reports in *The Times* of a parliamentary committee investigating child labour, and when

Clapham Sect of Evg Evangelical - Practical piety that integrated prayer + Bible study with social action

Value of emotions + imagination

when Wilberforce died 1833, Shaftesbury took over leadership

legacy eg NSPCA RSPCA

Michael Sadler, the politician who had been spearheading the campaign for reform, lost his seat in the 1832 General Election, Lord Ashley became the new leader of the factory reform movement in the House of Commons. Passionately evangelical, Shaftesbury was for the next fifty years to fight resolutely not just for the protection of children in factories and mines or employed as chimney sweeps, but also for the provision of education for the working classes, public health legislation, and proper care for the mentally ill.

The string of measures he helped to introduce is truly remarkable, beginning with the Factory Act of 1833, which made it illegal to employ children under nine in textile factories and for those between nine and thirteen to work for more than eight hours a day. The following year saw the introduction of the Chimney Sweeps Act, which banned the apprenticing of children over the age of nine (this was raised to sixteen in 1840) and the employment of any in actually cleaning chimneys before the age of fourteen. In 1840 Shaftesbury persuaded parliament to establish the Children's Employment Commission to consider the plight of poor children and to ensure they were being properly treated by their employers. Its report on children's working conditions in coal mines provoked a public outcry, many having been unaware that children and women were even employed in the mines, and later that year Shaftesbury was able to steer the Coal Mines Act through parliament, making it illegal for women, and children under ten, to work underground. There followed another Factory Act in 1847, which set ten hours a day as the maximum working time for women and children. Despite his efforts, employers frequently flouted the law, Shaftesbury reporting in 1863 that children as young as four and five were still being forced to work from six in the morning to ten at night in some British factories.

Lord Ashley also began a few 'Ragged Schools', designed to take working-class children off the street and to give them a basic education in reading and writing, and in the Bible. He later became chairman of the Ragged Schools Union, in which capacity he served for over forty years. In no small part, he contributed to the introduction in 1870 of compulsory education for children aged between five and ten, and later, in 1891, of free education in public schools.

Lord Ashley's passion for social justice sprang above all from his profound religious convictions. He focused strongly on the second coming of Christ, whose anticipated return filled him with an ardent desire to transform the lives of people, the country and the world. Thus, in an address to the House of Commons in 1840 he declared: 'The future hopes of a country must, under God, be laid in the character and condition of its children; however right it may be to attempt, it is almost fruitless to expect the reformation of its adults; as the sapling has been bent, so will it grow. The first step towards a cure is factory legislation. My grand object is to bring these children within the reach of education.' He later told his friend, the author and hymn writer Edwin Hodder: 'My religious views are not very popular but they are the views that have sustained and comforted me all through my life. I think a man's religion, if it is worth anything, should enter into every sphere of life, and rule his conduct in every relation.' It was such views that inspired this man, perhaps more than any other of his generation, to contribute immeasurably to improving the lives of thousands.

Bible verses

[handwritten: Just, justice, justly 100x – mainly OT – assocd with less of NT grace, mercy]

The Bible has countless passages that speak about the importance of social justice and its place at the heart of God's concern. Below are just a few of them. Read and reflect upon them before considering together the points for discussion raised afterwards.

[handwritten: Essential virtue of God is that just Deut 32:4]

Leviticus 19:15

[handwritten: Righteous called to mirror, for God loves the just Ps 37:28]

You shall not render an unjust judgement; you shall not be partial to the poor or defer to the great: with justice you shall judge your neighbour.

Deuteronomy 16:20

Justice, and only justice, you shall pursue, so that you may live and occupy the land that the Lord your God is giving you.

[handwritten: Justice in OT different from modern idea of fairness, treat cases alike]
[handwritten: ∴ Justice more than being fair – equals what is right 2 Chron 12:6]
[handwritten: ∴ Job suffers at Gods will despite righteousness + fact did not deserve]

25

Deuteronomy 27:19

Cursed be anyone who deprives the alien, the orphan, and the widow of justice. All the people shall say, 'Amen!'

Psalm 106:3

Happy are those who observe justice, who do righteousness at all times.

Psalm 140:12

I know that the Lord maintains the cause of the needy, and executes justice for the poor.

Proverbs 28:5

The evil do not understand justice, but those who seek the Lord understand it completely.

Proverbs 29:7

The righteous care about justice for the poor, but the wicked have no such concern.

Proverbs 31:9

The righteous know the rights of the poor; the wicked have no such understanding.

Isaiah 1:16, 17

Wash yourselves; make yourselves clean; remove the evil of your doings from before my eyes; cease to do evil, learn to do good; seek justice, rescue the oppressed, defend the orphan, plead for the widow.

Isaiah 10:1, 2

Ah, you who make iniquitous decrees, who write oppressive statutes, to turn aside the needy from justice and to rob the poor of my people of their right, that widows may be your spoil, and that you may make the orphans your prey!

Servant figure in Is. 42:1-4 epitomises strength + mercy of justice + love + deliverance

Isaiah 61:8

For I the Lord love justice, I hate robbery and wrongdoing; I will faithfully give them their recompense, and I will make an everlasting covenant with them.

Jeremiah 22:3

Thus says the Lord: Act with justice and righteousness, and deliver from the hand of the oppressor anyone who has been robbed. And do no wrong or violence to the alien, the orphan, and the widow, nor shed innocent blood in this place.

Ezekiel 34:15, 16

I myself will be the shepherd of my sheep, and I will make them lie down, says the Lord God. I will seek the lost, and I will bring back the strayed, and I will bind up the injured, and I will strengthen the weak, but the fat and the strong I will destroy. I will feed them with justice.

Zechariah 7:9, 10

Thus says the Lord of hosts: Render true judgements, show kindness and mercy to one another; do not oppress the widow, the orphan, the alien, or the poor; and do not devise evil in your hearts against one another.

Matthew 7:12

In everything do to others as you would have them do to you; for this is the law and the prophets.

Matthew 12:18

Here is my servant, whom I have chosen, my beloved, with whom my soul is well pleased. I will put my Spirit upon him, and he will proclaim justice to the Gentiles.

Matthew 23:23 (see also Luke 11:42)

Woe to you, scribes and Pharisees, hypocrites! For you tithe mint, dill, and cummin, and have neglected the weightier matters of the law: justice and mercy and faith. It is these you ought to have practised without neglecting the others.

Worship, rtly observance meaningless w/o justice

James 1:27

Religion that is pure and undefiled before God, the Father, is this: to care for orphans and widows in their distress, and to keep oneself unstained by the world.

James 5:1-5

Come now, you rich people, weep and wail for the miseries that are coming to you. Your riches have rotted, and your clothes are moth-eaten. Your gold and silver have rusted, and their rust will be evidence against you, and it will eat your flesh like fire. You have laid up treasure for the last days. Listen! The wages of the labourers who mowed your fields, which you kept back by fraud, cry out, and the cries of the harvesters have reached the ears of the Lord of hosts. You have lived on the earth in luxury and in pleasure; you have fattened your hearts on a day of slaughter.

1 John 3:17, 18

How does God's love abide in anyone who has the world's goods and sees a brother or sister in need and yet refuses help? Little children, let us love, not in word or speech, but in truth and action.

Discussion

- Which of the above passages speak most powerfully to you of the importance of social justice? Which do you find most challenging? How seriously do you take such words? Do you attempt to apply them in your life? Are there any aspects of the verses that you conveniently ignore?
- What issues of social justice do the production of cheap clothes and goods in sweatshops in Third World and developing countries pose for us today? How well informed are you about such issues?
- What issues of social justice do zero-hour and part-time contracts, the black market economy, erosion of workers' rights during the recent financial crisis, and the still-growing divide between rich and poor raise in our own country? Have any affected you personally?

- In what areas of social justice have you been aware of the Church speaking out in recent years? Does the Church involve itself enough in such issues? Can it take pride in the initiatives it has undertaken?
- Are there areas in which you'd like the Church to speak out more . . . or perhaps less?
- Can the Church avoid being involved in, or at least impinging on, party politics?
- What do you see as the key social issues facing our country, and our world, today? Is the Church sufficiently concerned about these? Could it, and should it, serve as a prophetic voice in today's world?

Quotes

Reflect individually on the following quotations for a moment, then discuss together which, if any, people found most helpful, and why. What point is each making? What lessons can be learned from them? What challenge do they present to us, personally, and to the Church in general.

- The opposite of poverty is not wealth. In too many places, the opposite of poverty is justice. (Bryan Stevenson)
- In keeping silent about evil, in burying it so deep within us that no sign of it appears on the surface, we are *implanting* it, and it will rise up a thousand fold in the future. When we neither punish nor reproach evildoers, we are not simply protecting their trivial old age, we are thereby ripping the foundations of justice from beneath new generations. (Aleksandr Solzhenitsyn)
- The world howls for social justice, but when it comes to social responsibility, you sometimes can't even hear crickets chirping. (Dean Koontz Odd Thomas)
- The ends you serve that are selfish will take you no further than yourself but the ends you serve that are for all, in common, will take you into eternity. (Marcus Garvey)

- The point is not that Jesus was a good guy who accepted everybody, and thus we should do the same (though that would be good). Rather, his teachings and behaviour reflect an alternative social vision. Jesus was not talking about how to be good and how to behave within the framework of a domination system. He was a critic of the domination system itself. (Marcus J. Borg)
- If you tremble with indignation at every injustice then you are a comrade of mine. (Ernesto Guevara)
- There is no doubt that the biblical concept of the Kingdom calls for a ministry to the suffering, the imprisoned, the oppressed, the hungry and whomever is dehumanised by an unjust society. In abstract, almost all of us can affirm this with enthusiasm. When it is the vocation, however, of one of our number to make this Gospel imperative, a matter demanding and requiring us to change our comfortable ways, then many of us fall away. The prophet has never been popular among his other contemporaries. He has been stoned, beheaded, crucified and shot. If not killed, we have been all too ready to vilify him or her in the name of God, little realising that it may well be God who sent the prophet to challenge our complacency. (Urban Tigner Holmes)
- The test of our progress is not whether we add more to the abundance of those who have much; it is whether we provide enough for those who have too little. (Franklin D. Roosevelt)

Final thoughts

We have come far in this country in terms of improving social justice for all, the welfare state, employment legislation and a raft of laws, rules and regulations safeguarding workers' rights and attempting to ensure a basic standard of living for all, yet we can never rest complacent. Rights can easily be eroded, poverty is a daily reality for many even in our own society, exploitation still exists, and many can still fall through the safety net, victims of ignorance or abuse. Looked at from a global perspective, issues of injustice, suffering and human need are all the more real, innumerable people still living in unimaginably awful conditions and often with a tragically short lifespan. Too easily we can push such situations out of sight, out of mind, yet we are part of an interdependent world in which their fates are inextricably interwoven with ours. We cannot put this world to rights on our own but neither can we turn our back on it as though it's no concern of ours. Ask yourself two simple questions – 'What am I doing?' and 'What could I be doing?', and resolve to make the answer to each as near as possible the same.

Closing prayer

Living God,
in a world of hunger and need,
give us hearts full of compassion;
in a world of evil and injustice,
give us a determination to make a difference;
in a world of greed and selfishness,
give us an open and generous spirit;
in a world of putting self first,
give us a genuine concern for others;
in a world of oppression and exploitation,
give us a yearning for justice.
Send us out to live and work for you.
Amen.

A voice for the sick – Florence Nightingale

Opening prayer

Lord Jesus Christ,
you speak of coming among us to make us whole –
whole in body, mind and spirit.
Thank you for the gift of health –
of being truly well in every part of our being –
and help us to understand more fully what that means.
Hear our prayer also for those who do not enjoy good health –
the sick,
injured,
disabled,
chronically or terminally ill –
and hear our prayer also for all those who seek to minister to
their needs –
doctors,
nurses,
consultants,
surgeons,
counsellors
therapists
and medical staff of all kinds.
Thank you for the ministry they perform
and inspire us in our turn to care more meaningfully for others,
offering what support and compassion we can
through Jesus Christ our Lord.
Amen.

Key passage

Then the king will say to those at his right hand, 'Come, you that
are blessed by my Father, inherit the kingdom prepared for you
from the foundation of the world; for I was hungry and you gave

me food, I was thirsty and you gave me something to drink, I was a stranger and you welcomed me, I was naked and you gave me clothing, I was sick and you took care of me, I was in prison and you visited me.' Then the righteous will answer him, 'Lord, when was it that we saw you hungry and gave you food, or thirsty and gave you something to drink? And when was it that we saw you a stranger and welcomed you, or naked and gave you clothing? And when was it that we saw you sick or in prison and visited you?' And the king will answer them, 'Truly I tell you, just as you did it to one of the least of these who are members of my family, you did it to me.'

Matthew 25:34-40

Introduction

'Health is not valued,' said the sixteenth-century English churchman and historian, Thomas Fuller, 'till sickness comes.' How right he was. When we are fit and well, health is something we take for granted, most of us blithely assuming that serious illness is something that happens to others, not to us. When we're unwell, however, it's a different story. Suddenly we realise how precarious is our hold on health, how sickness or disease can strike anyone, and how dependent we are at such times on those in our doctors' surgeries, health centres and hospitals. Not to have access to qualified and caring healthcare when we're genuinely unwell would be a frightening experience indeed; coping with the illness is quite enough in itself. Happily – for us in this country at least – treatment, nursing and so forth are available to us free at the point of need, and though the NHS is often the target of criticism and complaints, we are incredibly fortunate to have it. The fact that we do so is down, in part, to those like the woman we're going to be looking at in today's session, Florence Nightingale; those, in other words, who are committed to caring for others and whose example offers us a challenge to care for others in turn, albeit in more general ways.

Draughts activity

See the Appendix.

Study

Immortalised as 'the Lady of the Lamp', Florence Nightingale is one of those celebrated people we learn about very early in life, her name being forever associated with instituting qualified professional nursing. Before she came on the scene, the sick were typically treated at home by a family doctor – assuming that one could be afforded. The few hospitals that existed offered atrocious facilities and were typically poorly staffed. Of Glasgow Municipal Hospital in the mid-1850s, for example, its medical superintendent wrote, 'I admit that at present nursing is the last resource of female adversity. Slatternly widows, runaway wives, servants out of place, women bankrupt of fame or fortune from whatever cause, fall back on hospital nursing.' What nurses there were, in other words, were untrained, unqualified and frequently uncaring, doing their job because they had to rather than from any sense of vocation or innate compassion.

Army hospitals – in which Florence first made her name – were not much better. In these, nursing was mainly undertaken by disabled army veterans or, once again, by women who had fallen on hard times. Care was basic, to say the least; more often than not completely incompetent, patients being as likely to die as to recover as a result of their treatment. The hospitals were dirty and overcrowded, antiseptics non-existent, and bedding was rarely if ever washed, even after a patient had died.

In short, then, hospitals were not the sort of places in which reputable women were expected to work. So when Florence declared that she felt called by God to become a nurse, her well-to-do parents were appalled. It had all started back on 7 February 1837, when, just 17 years old, she had felt a keen sense that God was calling her to service – a sense of calling that only later, in 1850, crystallised into a clearer sense of vocation. This was reinforced when, on a visit to the Lutheran religious community at Kaiserswerth-am-Rhein in Germany, Florence saw first-hand how the sick were cared for in the hospital there, and she subsequently stayed on to receive four months' medical training.

After returning to England, Florence spent a short time as superintendent of the Institution for the Care of Sick Gentlewomen in Distressed Circumstances, in London, during which time, after the majority of the nurses walked out following an outbreak of cholera at the establishment, she won considerable regard for taking on many of the nursing duties herself. Then, when war broke out in the Crimea, Florence obtained permission from Sir Sidney Herbert – Secretary of War and also a family friend – to take a group of nurses there (10 Roman Catholic nuns, 14 Anglican nuns, and 14 other women of no particular religion). The conditions that met them were dreadful. Food was mouldy, water dirty, wards overcrowded; there were no operating tables and limited medical supplies; beds had no blankets, wards no sanitation and toilets no flushing system, resulting in an overpowering stench throughout the hospital. Once again, patients were far more likely to die of infection than from their wounds.

Despite opposition from some of her superiors, Florence wasted no time in addressing the issue, having the hospital scrubbed from top to bottom, after which survival rates improved spectacularly. Meanwhile, she spent just about every waking minute caring for the soldiers – dressing wounds, administering or supervising medical treatments, instructing nurses – earning herself the familiar sobriquet 'lady of the lamp' for her practice of patrolling the wards, lamp in hand, as she moved among them. Another name given to her, inspired by her compassionate ministry, was 'the Angel of the Crimea', and it was a title equally well deserved. Her work reduced the hospital's death rate by two-thirds, and she also instituted all kinds of services to improve the social welfare of patients. For Florence, nursing was not just about treating their medical condition but about making a difference to their whole lives.

After the war ended, Florence returned to England a national hero, but she had no interest in simply basking in the adulation. On the contrary, she lobbied parliament tirelessly for reform, not least through her 830-page report *Notes on Matters Affecting the Health, Efficiency and Hospital Administration of the British Army*, a publication that was to lead to the establishing of the Royal

Commission for the Health of the Army, in 1857, as well as of an Army Medical Staff Corps. In 1859, she published *Notes on Hospitals*, a book that explored how civilian hospitals should be run, and a year later, using a prize awarded to her by the British Government, Florence established a nursing school at St Thomas' Hospital in London, the first secular nursing school in the world. Her health was declining fast, undermined by her time in the Crimea, meaning that, from aged thirty-eight onwards, she was often bedridden, yet – in between caring for her dying father, then mother, then sister – she continued to campaign for improved healthcare for all, and countless of her suggestions were taken up not just in this country but across the world. So much of what we take for granted today is in fact due to her vision and dedication.

Here, then, is a woman of whom the Church can be proud; one that Christians can point to as a positive example of faith. So they should. Yet sadly – and profoundly illustrating Christianity's chequered history and the problems that still beset us – not all within the Church have done so, some having disagreed with her supposedly 'suspect', even 'heretical' views. Florence, for example, questioned the idea of a good God who could condemn souls to hell, and espoused instead the doctrine of universal salvation (when a dying young prostitute whom she was nursing spoke of her fear of hell, Florence reportedly responded, 'Oh, my girl, are you not now more merciful than the God you think you are going to? Yet the real God is far more merciful than any human creature ever was or can ever imagine'). She also strongly opposed discrimination against Christians of different denominations or those of other religions, believing that each had at least some insight into truth. Finally, she was frequently critical of organised religion, and particularly of its part in worsening the plight of the poor. Was she wrong in any of the above? Not in my book. Rather she seems in such things, as in her ministry in general, to have shown a level of openness that has all too often been lacking in Christian history. Her creed was pure and simple: genuine religion should show itself in practical care for and love of others. That's a lesson we all do well to learn.

Bible verses

The Bible has much to say on the healing ministry of Jesus, and speaks also of the healing ministry of the Church, but there are few passages concerned specifically with nursing or caring for the sick, per se. Perhaps the nearest we get to that is in Jesus' celebrated parable of the Good Samaritan:

Matthew 10:30-37

Jesus replied, 'A man was going down from Jerusalem to Jericho, and fell into the hands of robbers, who stripped him, beat him, and went away, leaving him half dead. Now by chance a priest was going down that road; and when he saw him, he passed by on the other side. So likewise a Levite, when he came to the place and saw him, passed by on the other side. But a Samaritan while travelling came near him; and when he saw him, he was moved with pity. He went to him and bandaged his wounds, having poured oil and wine on them. Then he put him on his own animal, brought him to an inn, and took care of him. The next day he took out two denarii, gave them to the innkeeper, and said, "Take care of him; and when I come back, I will repay you whatever more you spend." Which of these three, do you think, was a neighbour to the man who fell into the hands of the robbers?' He said, 'The one who showed him mercy.' Jesus said to him, 'Go and do likewise.'

Discussion

- Why do you think the Bible has so little to say on the subject of caring for the sick?
- How do you interpret passages of Scripture such us James 5:14, 15: 'Are any among you sick? They should call for the elders of the church and have them pray over them, anointing them with oil in the name of the Lord. The prayer of faith will save the sick, and the Lord will raise them up; and anyone who has committed sins will be forgiven'? Has modern medicine taken over the place of Christian healing? Do you still see a place for the ministry of healing today? If so, how does this fit in with established medical treatment?

- From what you've read, what do you feel were Florence Nightingale's most valuable contributions to nursing and to society at large, and what were her greatest qualities?
- In what ways can you show your care for others, especially the sick, infirm and unwell? Is your level of caring sometimes put to shame by that of non-Christians? What more could you, and the Church, be doing?
- What moral issues have modern medicine and nursing raised for today's Church? Does the Church approach these in the right way; i.e. in a spirit of love, compassion, openness and understanding, or does it seem sometimes to be dogmatically imposing its views on others?
- What does the questioning by some of Florence Nightingale's faith and beliefs say to you about the Church? Are doctrinal differences and so forth as much of a problem today as in her time? How far have these contributed to the chequered legacy of the Church, and do they continue still to do so?

Quotes

Reflect individually on the following quotations for a moment, then discuss together which, if any, people found most helpful, and why. What point is each making? What lessons can be learned from them? What challenge do they make to us, personally, and to the Church in general.

- Nursing is an art: and if it is to be made an art, it requires as exclusive a devotion, as hard a preparation, as any painter's or sculptor's work; for what is the having to do with dead canvas or dead marble, compared with having to do with the living body, the temple of God's spirit? It is one of the Fine Arts: I had almost said, the finest of Fine Arts. (Florence Nightingale)
- Never believe that a few caring people can't change the world. For, indeed, that's all who ever have. (Margaret Mead)
- The wish for healing has always been half of health. (Lucius Annaeus Seneca)
- Constant attention by a good nurse may be just as important as a major operation by a surgeon. (Dag Hammarskjold)

- To array a man's will against his sickness is the supreme art of medicine. (Henry Ward Beecher)
- The greatest healing therapy is friendship and love. (Hubert Humphrey)
- The art of medicine consists of keeping the patient amused, while nature heals the disease. (Voltaire)
- Kindness can transform someone's dark moment with a blaze of light. You'll never know how much your caring matters. Make a difference for another today. (Amy Leigh Mercree)
- The trained nurse has become one of the great blessings of humanity, taking a place beside the physician and the priest. (William Osler)
- [In sickness] your heaviest artillery will be your will to live. Keep that big gun going. (Norman Cousins)
- Healing is a matter of time, but it is sometimes also a matter of opportunity. (Hippocrates)
- The closest thing to being cared for is to care for someone else. (Carson McCullers)
- If you hear that a sick man is in need of hot soup, I counsel you to wake up from your ecstasy and warm the soup for him. Leave God to serve God. (John Ruysbroeck)
- Caring is the essence of nursing. (Jean Watson)
- The most important thing when ill, is to never lose heart. (Vladimir Ilyich Lenin)
- Love does not cost anything. Kind words and deeds do not cost anything. The real beauty of the world is equal for everyone to see. It was given by God equally to all, without restrictions. Everyone was given a beautiful vehicle in which to express love to others. Feelings are free to express and give to ourselves and each other through our willingness to give and care. (Carla Jo Masterson)
- There are no such things as incurable, there are only things for which man has not found a cure. (Bernard Mannes Baruch)
- Too often we underestimate the power of a touch, a smile, a kind word, a listening ear, an honest compliment, or the smallest act of caring, all of which have the potential to turn a life around. (Leo Buscaglia)

- How is it possible that suffering that is neither my own nor of my concern should immediately affect me as though it were my own, and with such force that is moves me to action? (Arthur Schopenhauer)

Final thoughts

There is, I believe, a particularly powerful challenge to every Christian posed by the nickname given to Florence Nightingale: 'lady of the lamp'. It calls to mind that iconic painting by William Holman Hunt, *The Light of the World* – a simply yet powerful portrayal of Jesus standing at the door of someone's life as he seeks to fill them with light. None of us, of course, can begin to offer illumination anywhere near as bright or enduring as he does, but we are called to shed light nonetheless: 'In the same way, let your light shine before others, so that they may see your good works and give glory to your Father in heaven' (Matthew 5:16). That's what Florence Nightingale did, her compassion and dedication shedding a ray of sunshine upon those wrestling with the darkness of ill health. And that's what each of us are called, in our own way, to do in turn, however modest may be the light we're able to bring. If, like Florence, we focused more on that and less on doctrinal differences, how much more effective, and less chequered, our witness might be.

Closing prayer

Loving God,
thank you for those who care about their fellow human beings;
those who are ready to give of their time, energy, skills or money
to reach out to them in their need
and to offer a ministry of love and healing.
Thank you for those,
both within and beyond the Church,
who strive to bring strength,
solace,
support
and succour to all battling with ill health.

Inspire us through their example to care more about others in turn
and to respond practically to their needs.
Help us to live more fully as your people,
in a way that truly brings honour to you
and blessing to others.
Amen.

A voice for the voiceless – Martin Luther King

Opening prayer

Living God,
thank you for the place we have in your heart;
for the way you value us as individuals,
each of us being precious in your sight.
Thank you for the place we have in society:
the right to be ourselves,
respected for who we are,
each entitled to freedom of speech and opinion.
Help us to recognise what all that means,
and to rejoice in it,
understanding what we owe to generations before us
who have secured a voice and rights that we too easily take
for granted.
Speak to us today through the example of those who have stood
up for the voiceless,
and who have campaigned for the dignity and freedom of
the oppressed.
Raise up more people like them to challenge the evils and
injustices of today,
and give us the courage and vision we need to speak out as
your people
and to offer support for their cause,
working as best we can for the dawn of your kingdom
on earth as it is in heaven.
Amen.

Key passage

There is no longer Jew or Greek, there is no longer slave or free, there is no longer male and female; for all of you are one in Christ Jesus.

Galatians 3:28

Introduction

Living today in the UK, we may find our world less than perfect, but it's a good deal more perfect than it would have been in centuries past. Go back 200 years and children were working in mines, workers being paid a pittance in newly emerging factories, and countless people living in abject poverty. Go back just 100 years and women were still campaigning for the vote, the health service and welfare state were undreamt of, and the First World War was claiming the lives of millions. Happily, we live today in an age when at least some of the evils that have scarred human relationships across the years have been tackled. But we cannot be complacent for a moment. Many hard-won gains could easily be lost, prejudice being more deeply rooted in society than we might imagine, as is evidenced by the intolerant nationalism daily fostered by certain newspaper headlines and right-wing parties. Today we focus on a man who took on one of the most enduring, destructive and iniquitous prejudices of all time: that of racism. The man, of course, was the great American civil rights campaigner, Martin Luther King.

Draughts activity

See the Appendix.

Study

His father and grandfather having both been Baptist ministers heavily involved in the US civil rights movement, Martin Luther King was born on 15 January 1929 in Atlanta, Georgia, to Martin Luther, Sr and Alberta, a schoolteacher. In 1954, after training at Morehouse College in Atlanta, and then undertaking postgraduate research in Pennsylvania and Boston – where he met and married his wife Coretta Scott, whom he married in 1953 – he became pastor of Dexter Avenue Baptist Church in Montgomery, Alabama – the city where, notoriously, Rosa Parks was arrested after refusing to give up her seat to a white man on a bus (seats on buses at the time were divided between those for blacks and whites). It was her arrest that set King upon a path of protests and resistance that was to lead finally to his death yet contribute, perhaps more than any other, to a change of attitudes within American society and beyond.

Together with various friends, King organised a boycott of buses by the 17,000 black people of Montgomery, until after 13 months, unable to sustain the resulting financial losses, the Montgomery Bus Company capitulated and accepted the integration of all passengers. It was a victory for the civil rights movement, though one not won without personal cost, King being arrested during the protest and his home firebombed.

Subsequent to the campaign, King was introduced to Mahatma Gandhi's principle of non-violent action by Bayard Rustin and Harris Wofford, prominent civil rights campaigners, as a result of which, with fellow activists, he established the Southern Christian Leadership Conference in 1957, an organisation that took as its motto 'Not one hair of one head of one person should be harmed.' King expanded on the principle of non-violent resistance in his book *Stride Toward Freedom*, published in 1958, and shortly afterwards, inspired by his words, a group of black students in Greensboro, North Carolina, staged a sit-in at the restaurant in their local Woolworth's store, which, like others, refused to serve black people. Despite intimidation and violence, more and more black students joined in, refusing to defend themselves but gradually filling all the seats in the restaurant. The tactic was so effective that, before long, similar student sit-ins and protests were taking place all over America's Deep South. Campaigns were successfully launched against segregation in public parks, swimming pools, museums, transport, churches, theatres and beaches.

Less successful, though, was an attempt in 1963 to end segregation at lunch counters in Birmingham, Alabama. Birmingham's residents were notoriously hostile to any form of desegregation, the city having earned the nickname 'Bombingham' due to the number of attacks on the homes of black people and activists there, so it was no surprise that King, together with many of his supporters, soon found himself arrested and jailed. It was while he was being held in solitary confinement that King wrote his celebrated 'Letter from Birmingham Jail', in which he replied to criticism of his actions from many of Birmingham's white clergy: 'For years now,' he wrote, 'I have heard the word "Wait!" This "Wait" has almost always meant "Never".'

When he was finally released from prison, King helped to launch the Children's Crusade in Birmingham, thousands of schoolchildren and students marching from 2–5 May 1963 in the streets in what turned out to be one of the biggest civil rights protests held so far. When police responded with baton charges, dogs and high-pressure fire hoses, condemnation followed from across the world, and King swiftly became an international hero.

Shortly afterwards, King delivered his immortal 'I have a dream' speech to the mass crowds who had taken part in the March on Washington for Jobs and Freedom on 28 August 1963. His words, to over 200,000 people gathered at the Lincoln Memorial, have gone down in history, bringing hope and inspiration to the black community of America who had for so long been denied a voice:

> I say to you today, my friends, so even though we face the difficulties of today and tomorrow, I still have a dream. It is a dream deeply rooted in the American dream.
>
> I have a dream that one day this nation will rise up and live out the true meaning of its creed: 'We hold these truths to be self-evident; that all men are created equal.'
>
> I have a dream that my four little children will one day live in a nation where they will not be judged by the colour of their skin but by the content of their character.
>
> I have a dream that one day every valley shall be exalted, every hill and mountain shall be made low, the rough places will be made plain, and the crooked places will be made

straight, and the glory of the Lord shall be revealed, and all flesh shall see it together.

This is our hope. This is the faith that I will go back to the South with. With this faith we will be able to hew out of the mountain of despair a stone of hope. With this faith we will be able to transform the jangling discords of our nation into a beautiful symphony of brotherhood.

With this faith we will be able to work together, to pray together, to struggle together, to go to jail together, to stand up for freedom together, knowing that we will be free one day.

Just a few weeks after he uttered those memorable words, four young girls were killed in a bomb blast in a Birmingham church, graphically emphasising the divide between vision and reality.

In 1964, King was awarded the Nobel Peace Prize and the Civil Rights Act was passed, followed in 1965 by that of the Voting Rights Act. For the next two years, King turned his attention to the north of America, with limited success, and then, on 3 April 1968, came that moment which was to shock the world. While he was in Memphis, Tennessee, in support of striking sanitation workers, Martin was shot dead on his hotel balcony, reportedly by a crazed lone gunman, James Earl Ray, though many have suggested that the hand of the authorities, or other of his enemies, lay behind it. The previous night he had finished a speech with words almost as famous as those from his 'I have a dream' address:

Well, I don't know what will happen now; we've got some difficult days ahead. But it really doesn't matter with me now, because I've been to the mountaintop. And I don't mind. Like anybody, I would like to live a long life – longevity has its place. But I'm not concerned about that now. I just want to do God's will. And He's allowed me to go up to the mountain. And I've looked over, and I've seen the promised land. I may not get there with you. But I want you to know tonight, that we, as a people, will get to the promised land. So I'm happy tonight; I'm not worried about anything; I'm not fearing any man. Mine eyes have seen the glory of the coming of the Lord.

Effectively, he had given his life for the sake of the black oppressed minority. The voice of the voiceless had been silenced, yet in death it spoke louder than ever.

Bible verses

The Bible doesn't say much specifically on the subject of racism, yet many verses can be related directly to it. Read and reflect upon the following before considering together the points for discussion raised afterwards.

Genesis 1:27

So God created humankind in his image, in the image of God he created them; male and female he created them.

1 Samuel 16:7

But the Lord said to Samuel, 'Do not look on his appearance or on the height of his stature, because I have rejected him; for the Lord does not see as mortals see; they look on the outward appearance, but the Lord looks on the heart.'

Matthew 7:12

'In everything do to others as you would have them do to you; for this is the law and the prophets.'

John 7:24

'Do not judge by appearances, but judge with right judgement.'

John 13:34

'I give you a new commandment, that you love one another. Just as I have loved you, you also should love one another.'

Acts 10:34, 35

Then Peter began to speak to them: 'I truly understand that God shows no partiality, but in every nation anyone who fears him and does what is right is acceptable to him.'

Romans 2:11

For God shows no partiality.

Romans 10:12

For there is no distinction between Jew and Greek; the same Lord is Lord of all and is generous to all who call on him.

1 Corinthians 12:12, 13

For just as the body is one and has many members, and all the members of the body, though many, are one body, so it is with Christ. For in the one Spirit we were all baptised into one body – Jews or Greeks, slaves or free – and we were all made to drink of one Spirit.

Colossians 3:9-11

Do not lie to one another, seeing that you have stripped off the old self with its practices and have clothed yourselves with the new self, which is being renewed in knowledge according to the image of its creator. In that renewal there is no longer Greek and Jew, circumcised and uncircumcised, barbarian, Scythian, slave and free; but Christ is all and in all!

James 2:9

But if you show partiality, you commit sin and are convicted by the law as transgressors.

1 John 2:9

Whoever says, 'I am in the light', while hating a brother or sister, is still in the darkness.

Discussion

- What examples of racism can be found in the Bible? Could the Egyptians' oppression of the Israelites be seen as an example of it? Can the Israelites be exempt from the charge in their conquest of the Promised Land? Think also of the antipathy of the Judeans towards the Samaritans, and vice versa.

- What are the underlying causes of racism? Why does it still exist in certain institutions and sections of society? Where is it most prevalent in our country today? Has racism been fanned by the recent global economic problems? Do you think this has led to new manifestations of racism; for example, stereotypical assumptions concerning the motivations of Eastern Europeans and the like, or even simply a general suspicion of 'foreigners taking our jobs' or 'coming to scrounge of benefits'? Has the so-called 'war on terror', and the perceived threat of terrorism, contributed to racist attitudes? If so, in what way?
- Which Bible passages, for you, speak most effectively against racism? Why?
- What was it about Martin Luther King, do you think, that made him such an effective and powerful leader of the civil rights movement? What lessons can we learn from him?
- According to Martin Luther King, 'A man who won't die for something is not fit to live.' Do you agree with that sentiment? What things, if necessary, would you be willing to die for?
- Why do you think some US white clergy may have criticised and opposed Martin Luther King's activism? What does this say to us about the Church? Does racism still exist in the Church today? If so in what ways? How far is this reflected in the structures and hierarchy of the Church?

Quotes

Reflect individually on the following quotations – all from Martin Luther King – for a moment, then discuss together which, if any, people found most helpful (refer back also to King's speech's above). What point is each making, and why? What lessons can be learned from them? What challenge do they make to us, personally, and to the Church in general?

- He who passively accepts evil is as much involved in it as he who helps to perpetrate it. He who accepts evil without protesting against it is really cooperating with it.
- The time is always right to do what is right.

- The ultimate measure of a man is not where he stands in moments of comfort and convenience, but where he stands at times of challenge and controversy.
- An individual has not started living until he can rise above the narrow confines of his individualistic concerns to the broader concerns of all humanity.
- Every man must decide whether he will walk in the light of creative altruism or in the darkness of destructive selfishness.
- Injustice anywhere is a threat to justice everywhere. When we discover this, we are less prone to hate our enemies.
- Our scientific power has outrun our spiritual power. We have guided missiles and misguided men.
- Love is the only force capable of transforming an enemy into a friend.
- Life's most persistent and urgent question is, 'What are you doing for others?'
- Our lives begin to end the day we become silent about things that matter.
- In the End, we will remember not the words of our enemies, but the silence of our friends.
- Take the first step in faith. You don't have to see the whole staircase, just take the first step.
- I have decided to stick with love. Hate is too great a burden to bear.
- We must learn to live together as brothers or perish together as fools.
- Change does not roll in on the wheels of inevitability, but comes through continuous struggle. And so we must straighten our backs and work for our freedom. A man can't ride you unless your back is bent.
- Darkness cannot drive out darkness; only light can do that. Hate cannot drive out hate; only love can do that.
- Eleven o'clock on Sunday morning . . . is the most segregated hour in Christian America.

Final thoughts

Christians have by no means been innocent of racism across the centuries as so tragically evidenced by apartheid in South Africa, nor are they always so today. Indeed, as recently as 1979 the Church of England was accused, in a Daily Telegraph report (17 June) of being institutionally racist, and the same charge could equally be levelled against other denominations. On this issue, as in many, the legacy of the Church is a mixture of good and bad. Martin Luther King is categorically an example of the good: a man who had the courage to stand up for his convictions, and for a fundamental truth at the heart of the Christian faith, in the face of hostility, persecution, intimidation and, eventually, the ultimate cost. Most of us will not have even a fraction of such courage, nor, happily, will we be called upon to show it. But there may well be times when we need to make a stand against prejudice in one or other of its many shapes and forms, including perhaps that of racism. Will we be ready to do so, boldly and unequivocally, when that challenge comes?

Closing prayer

Loving God,
forgive the racism that has scarred our world across the centuries –
the hatred it has engendered,
persecution it has led to,
injustices and misery it has caused,
violence, murder and genocide it has been used to justify.
Forgive the racism that has scarred the Church over the years:
persecution of Jews and Muslims,
the iniquity of apartheid,
innate white elitism,
rank prejudice and discrimination.
Reach out to those who continue to be victims of racism today,
being intimidated,
discriminated against,
victimised,
abused,
suffering on account of the colour of their skin or place of origin.

Prosper, we pray, the work of all those who work to combat racism,
and break down the barriers of prejudice that keep people apart,
so that everyone,
everywhere,
may learn to recognise, respect and value the common humanity
we share.
Amen.

Especial need for Christians
Quote Jim Wallis 3+8

Relig persecution

Homosexuality and Anglican Commun

Ephesians 4 : 1-6 , 22-24 [207]
Unity in Body of Christ
enter new life in likeness of God
SESSION FIVE

A voice for peace and reconciliation – Nelson Mandela

Opening prayer

Loving God,
you call us to seek peace,
to do everything in our power to make it happen:
to turn the other cheek,
love our enemies,
pray for those who persecute us,
forgive those who do us wrong.
Yet we find it so hard,
for our natural inclination is to lash out at those who hurt us,
to avenge ourselves,
to seek an eye for an eye and a tooth for a tooth.
We find it hard to let go of resentment,
particularly when we have been genuinely wronged,
and it doesn't seem right that evil and injustice should
go unpunished,
its perpetrators escaping scot-free.
Yet we know that the way of revenge and recrimination leads
only to more of the same:
to an escalating spiral of hatred and division.
Speak to us today through those who have had the humility,
vision and courage
to pursue a different way:
the way of Christ –
those who have not just talked of forgiveness
but have shown it in practice,
and in so doing have healed wounds,
establishing genuine peace and reconciliation.
Teach us, in whatever ways we can, to do the same,
and so to help shape the new heaven and earth you desire for all.
Amen.

*† We profess to love God
Let us ask God to shew us how
to love our neighbour
ask selves what division in world so ma
~~problems~~ of us. Ask for grace to [illegible]
with othe[illegible]*

Key passage

If it is possible, so far as it depends on you, live peaceably with all. *with othe[illegible]*

Romans 12: 18

†

*1960 Rem despair at Sharpeville
Bloodbath of revenge only future ed sc*

Introduction

If ever there was an answer to the often-stated suggestion that miracles don't happen today, it must surely lie in what's happened to South Africa in the past twenty-five years. Countless people longed to see the end of apartheid in that country, many of them having worked long and hard to achieve it, but, if they were honest, many were also profoundly nervous of it ever happening, for one simple reason: could it possibly come about without a bloodbath? First, could the white minority ever be persuaded to give up their hold on power by anything other than an armed uprising that would inevitably see wholesale slaughter? And second, even if that could somehow be achieved, would it then be possible to restrain the black majority from indulging in an orgy of recrimination as they looked to pay back old scores and suitably punish their long-time oppressors? Most observers secretly felt it was an impossible situation. After all, had we ourselves been subjected to the humiliation and injustice that the black majority endured for so long in South Africa, we would certainly have expected to get back our pound of flesh. It seemed unlikely in the extreme that black and white people would ever be able to coexist peaceably in that troubled land. Yet that is precisely what has happened, the expected carnage never materialising and South Africa having been truly transformed. That this is so is due in large part to the staggering contribution of one man in particular. It is not for nothing that the late Nelson Mandela, former South African president, is revered across the world as one of the few truly great figures of recent times. He stands as a colossus over modern history – an example of a new kind of politics and of everything that can be achieved through it. And, though less feted, alongside him should probably stand another name: that of Mandela's friend and confidant Archbishop Desmond Tutu, whose unflinching and courageous stand against apartheid, coupled

*Dutch Reformed Church
– condemned by WCC* ⊗

*But patient Christian witness in S Af. for decades
Alan Paton, Trevor Huddleston* ⟶

with his subsequent work as chair of the Peace and Reconciliation Committee established after its demise, helped to fashion the new era we see in that country today. Their work, their example, their voices, stand as a continuing clarion call to us all.

Draughts activity

See the Appendix.

Study

Great-grandson to the chief of the Thembu people in South Africa's modern Eastern Cape province, Nelson Mandela was born in the small village of Mvezo, but grew up in the even smaller village of Qunu after his father – who died when Nelson was aged just nine – lost his tribal status in a dispute with a local magistrate. On his father's death, Nelson was adopted by Chief Jongintaba Dalindyebo, the acting regent of the Thembu, and taken to the royal residence at Mqhekezweni, where he was raised as one of the chief's own sons. Schooled for high office, he eventually studied at the University College of Fort Hare, the premier university for black students in South Africa, but was expelled for taking part in a student protest. Learning that his furious step-father was planning an arranged marriage for him, Nelson ran away to Johannesburg where, supporting himself through various jobs, he completed his BA and went on to the University of Witwatersrand in Johannesburg to study law.

Having long been interested in African history, Nelson became involved in the anti-apartheid movement and joined the African National Congress (ANC) in 1942, through which he helped to orchestrate a long-running campaign of non-violent protest and civil disobedience against South Africa's segregation laws. Tensions rose to a head following the infamous Sharpeville Massacre of 1960, in which police killed 69 unarmed people in a protest against pass laws. Mandela, together with countless fellow protestors, found himself detained during a government-declared state of emergency, and both the ANC and the more militant Pan Africanist Congress were outlawed.

57

At this point, even Nelson Mandela came to feel that change could only come about through armed struggle, and he helped to found the MK (short for *Umkhonto we Sizwe*, meaning 'spear of the nation'), a guerrilla unit specialising in sabotage. A year later, in 1962, he was arrested for leading a national workers' strike and sentenced to five years in prison, this subsequently being increased in 1964 to life imprisonment for his involvement with the MK. In total, he was to spend twenty-seven years in prison, eighteen of those on Robben Island. During that time, campaigners lobbied globally for his release, growing international pressure and sanctions, coupled with mounting civil unrest, finally forcing the hand of South African president F.W. de Klerk, who – on 11 February 1990 – lifted the ban on the ANC and ordered that Mandela be set free. Together the two men entered into negotiations, culminating in 1994 with multiracial elections that saw Mandela elected as the country's first black president.

It was at this point that the world began to get the full measure of the man, hinted at in words he spoke on his release: 'As I walked out the door toward the gate that would lead to my freedom, I knew if I didn't leave my bitterness and hatred behind, I'd still be in prison.' Sure enough, instead of him instigating gleeful reprisals, as many had expected when he took office, or pursuing a path of recriminations against white South Africans, Mandela did the opposite, seeking from the beginning to build bridges and unite the nation. A key part in achieving that was his establishing of the Truth and Reconciliation Commission, charged on the one hand with investigating past human rights abuses and making reparations to victims, but on the other with promoting healing and forgiveness. A key figure in that process was Archbishop Desmond Tutu, the first chairman of the Commission and a long-standing campaigner against apartheid. 'Instead of revenge and retribution,' he said,

> this new nation chose to tread the difficult path of confession, forgiveness, and reconciliation . . . And we have been richly blessed to have had at such a critical time in our history a Nelson Mandela. He was imprisoned for 27 years; most

expected that when he emerged, he would be riddled with a lust for retribution. But the world has been amazed; instead of spewing calls for revenge, he urged his own people to work for reconciliation – and invited his former jailer to attend his presidential inauguration as a VIP guest . . . We have been appalled at the depths of depravity revealed by the testimonies before the Truth and Reconciliation Commission. Yes, we human beings have a remarkable capacity for evil – we have refined ways of being mean and nasty to one another. There have been genocides, holocausts, slavery, racism, wars, oppression and injustice.

But that, mercifully, is not the whole story about us. We were exhilarated as we heard people who had suffered grievously, who by rights should have been baying for the blood of their tormentors, utter words of forgiveness, reveal an extraordinary willingness to work for reconciliation, demonstrating magnanimity and nobility of spirit.

Yes, wonderfully, exhilaratingly, we have this extraordinary capacity for good. Fundamentally, we are good; we are made for love, for compassion, for caring, for sharing, for peace and reconciliation, for transcendence, for the beautiful, for the true and the good.

A hugely powerful and poignant moment in South Africa's transformation came when the Springbok rugby team – which had been such a symbol of white authority during the apartheid years that most black South Africans would support the opposing team instead – reached the final of the 1995 Rugby World Cup. Into a packed stadium, Mandela walked out on to the pitch wearing the green Springbok shirt and cap, and shook hands with the South African team, most of whom were white. It was a graphic demonstration of his commitment to new beginnings, for which he continued to work tirelessly, even after standing down as president in 1999.

Can we claim Nelson Mandela as an example of a Christian working for good? He never made a show of his faith, and the exact nature of his convictions remains unclear, but he seems to have been sustained by a profound commitment throughout his life. Words he spoke at the 1994 Zionist Christian Church's Easter Conference not only point to that commitment but also sum up the challenge Mandela brought to both South Africa and the whole world:

[handwritten: Evangelion - manifesto for radical change]

> The Good News borne by our risen Messiah who chose not one race, who chose not one country, who chose not one language, who chose not one tribe, who chose all of humankind!
>
> Each Easter marks the rebirth of our faith. It marks the victory of our risen Saviour over the torture of the cross and the grave. *[handwritten: Suffering God]*
>
> Our Messiah, who came to us in the form of a mortal man, but who by his suffering and crucifixion attained immortality.
>
> Our Messiah, born like an outcast in a stable, and executed like criminal on the cross. *[handwritten: Form of execution for treason, subversion of the natural order]*
>
> Our Messiah, whose life bears testimony to the truth that there is no shame in poverty: those who should be ashamed are they who impoverish others.
>
> Whose life testifies to the truth that there is no shame in being persecuted: those who should be ashamed are they who persecute others.
>
> Whose life proclaims the truth that there is no shame in being conquered: those who should be ashamed are they who conquer others.
>
> Whose life testifies to the truth that there is no shame in being dispossessed: those who should be ashamed are they who dispossess others.
>
> Whose life testifies to the truth that there is no shame in being oppressed: those who should be ashamed are they who oppress others.

There we see not just a voice for peace and reconciliation, but the voice of a prophet, whose message continues to confront our world today, calling us to a new way of living and new way of loving: the way of Christ. Do that genuinely and we'll leave a legacy of which the world will genuinely sit up and take notice.

[handwritten: Common Humanity of Creation is basis of human rights / Humanist Society]

Bible verses

The Bible has much to say on matters of peace and reconciliation. Read and reflect upon the following before considering together the points for discussion raised afterwards.

Psalm 34:14

Depart from evil, and do good; seek peace, and pursue it.

Proverbs 16:7

When the ways of people please the Lord, he causes even their enemies to be at peace with them.

Isaiah 2:4 (see also Micah 4:3)

He shall judge between the nations, and shall arbitrate for many peoples; they shall beat their swords into ploughshares, and their spears into pruning-hooks; nation shall not lift up sword against nation, neither shall they learn war any more.

Isaiah 52:7

How beautiful upon the mountains are the feet of the messenger who announces peace, who brings good news, who announces salvation, who says to Zion, 'Your God reigns.'

Matthew 5:39

'But I say to you, Do not resist an evildoer. But if anyone strikes you on the right cheek, turn the other also.'

Matthew 6:14

'For if you forgive others their trespasses, your heavenly Father will also forgive you.'

Luke 6:27, 28

'But I say to you that listen, Love your enemies, do good to those who hate you, bless those who curse you, pray for those who abuse you.'

Luke 6:37

'Do not judge, and you will not be judged; do not condemn, and you will not be condemned. Forgive, and you will be forgiven.'

Romans 14:19

Let us then pursue what makes for peace and for mutual edification.

Ephesians 4:31, 32

Context is new life in Christ
4:25 – 5:2

Put away from you all bitterness and wrath and anger and wrangling and slander, together with all malice, and be kind to one another, tender-hearted, forgiving one another, as God in Christ has forgiven you.

Colossians 3:12, 13

As God's chosen ones, holy and beloved, clothe yourselves with compassion, kindness, humility, meekness, and patience. Bear with one another and, if anyone has a complaint against another, forgive each other; just as the Lord has forgiven you, so you also must forgive.

Hebrews 12:14

Pursue peace with everyone, and the holiness without which no one will see the Lord.

1 Peter 3:11

Let them turn away from evil and do good; let them seek peace and pursue it.

Discussion

- How far is it possible to follow the biblical injunctions above, particularly the challenge of Jesus to love our enemies, turn the other cheek and so forth? Does Nelson Mandela's promotion of reconciliation help you to believe that this way is a viable option rather than idealistic dream?

- Was Nelson Mandela justified in advocating a move away from non-violent protest to armed resistance? Would change in South Africa ever have been possible without this? Are you against taking up arms altogether, or are there circumstances in which you believe this might be necessary?
- What issues are involved in effecting reconciliation? What are the obstacles that must be faced? On a personal level, have you faced the challenge of seeking reconciliation with someone? Were you able to achieve this? If so, how? What do you find hardest in forgiving someone who has wronged you? How good are you at saying sorry when you have wronged others?
- In what parts of the world do issues of peace and reconciliation still urgently need to be addressed? What are the key factors preventing change in such places?
- What, for you, was Nelson Mandela's most significant contribution to South Africa and the world, and what were his greatest qualities?

Quotes

Reflect individually on the following quotations for a moment, then discuss together which, if any, people found most helpful, and why. What point is each making? What lessons can be learned from them? What challenge do they make to us, personally, and to the Church in general.

- We must be the change we wish to see in the world. (Mahatma Gandhi)
- We are all one – or at least we should be – and it is our job, our duty, and our great challenge to fight the voices of division and seek the salve of reconciliation. (Roy Barnes)
- Peace comes from being able to contribute the best that we have, and all that we are, towards creating a world that supports everyone. But it is also securing the space for others to contribute the best that they have and all that they are. (Hafsat Abiola)
- Reconciliation requires changes of heart and spirit, as well as social and economic change. It requires symbolic as well as practical action. (Malcolm Fraser)

- Better than a thousand hollow words is one word that brings peace. (Buddha)
- In the aftermath of any war or genocide, healing and reconciliation are ultimate aspirations. (Janine di Giovanni)
- The world is not dialectical – it is sworn to extremes, not to equilibrium, sworn to radical antagonism, not to reconciliation or synthesis. This is also the principle of evil. (Jean Baudrillard)
- Peace is the work of justice indirectly, insofar as justice removes the obstacles to peace; but it is the work of charity (love) directly, since charity, according to its very notion, causes peace. (Thomas Aquinas)
- We must develop and maintain the capacity to forgive. He who is devoid of the power to forgive is devoid of the power to love. There is some good in the worst of us and some evil in the best of us. When we discover this, we are less prone to hate our enemies. (Martin Luther King)
- The practice of peace and reconciliation is one of the most vital and artistic of human actions. (Nhat Hanh)
- The work of community, love, reconciliation, restoration is the work we cannot leave up to politicians. This is the work we are all called to do. (Shane Claiborne)
- Teach this triple truth to all: a generous heart, kind speech, and a life of service and compassion are the things which renew humanity. (Buddha)
- Chimps are very quick to have a sudden fight or aggressive episode, but they're equally as good at reconciliation. (Jane Goodall)
- We used to wonder where war lived, what it was that made it so vile. And now we realise that we know where it lives, that it is inside ourselves. (Albert Camus)

Final thoughts

A force for good: that's what we've seen not just in the example of Nelson Mandela but in each of the five people we've focused on in the course of this book, and there are many others we could add to the list. None of them would have seen themselves as a voice of the Church, nor of Christians in general – they were simply working out their faith in the way that seemed right to them. But through so doing they demonstrate what Christian commitment can help to inspire – a legacy to be proud of and to learn from. No doubt all five had their faults, and critics almost certainly will pick holes in their actions and life stories, but they contributed nonetheless towards the building of a better world. Will anyone be able to say the same of us? Our opportunities to make a difference will be much more limited, influencing the lives of perhaps a handful at most rather than many, but that doesn't matter. What's important is that we, too, seek to work for good wherever and whenever we can, so that, chequered though it may be, the legacy of the Church may point a little more *towards* Christ, and a little less *away* from him.

Closing prayer

Lord Jesus Christ,
we look forward at this time of year to your coming again;
your return on earth to establish your kingdom,
and to bring in a new era of peace, justice and blessing for all.
Teach us not simply to talk of such things,
but to seek to make them happen;
to do whatever we can through our life and witness to help bring your kingdom closer,
bringing a foretaste of heaven here on earth.
Though what we can achieve alone may be all too small,
remind us that,
in partnership with all your people,
it may be greater than we may imagine.
Challenge us, then,
guide, inspire and help us,
to live in such a way that does not give conflicting signals
but speaks simply and solely of your love –
a love that extends unfailingly and unconditionally to all.
Amen.

Appendix

Below are lists of some of the good and bad things the Church has been involved in across the centuries (you may wish to research online and add to these). Write or print these off individually on draughts-piece-sized circles, and affix them to the base of draughts pieces. Invite participants to play a game of draughts against each other during the activity session, turning over pieces as they are taken as a reminder of the Church's chequered legacy and noting the characters of incidents revealed.

Look up details of any of these events/people you're not familiar with and briefly give details after the activity of those that people have turned up, perhaps inviting brief comments and discussion, but don't allow the session to get bogged down at this stage.

The bad

The Pogroms
The Irish troubles
Persecution of 'witches'
House arrest of Galileo
The Inquisition
Persecution of 'heretics'
The St Bartholomew's Day (Huguenot) Massacre
Support for the slave trade
The Albanian Genocide
Persecution of Catholics
Persecution of Protestants
Burning of Thomas Cranmer
Burning of Bishop Nicholas Ridley
Burning of Archbishop Hugh Latimer
Posthumous burning of John Wycliffe at the stake
Burning of Joan of Arc
Burning of Jan Hus
Burning of William Tyndale
Banning of translation of the Bible from Greek, Hebrew and Latin

Sale of indulgences
Trade in religious relics
Torture and murder of the Knights Templar
The Münster Rebellion
Massacre of the Jews of in York (1190)
Forced conversion of 'pagans'
The conquest of South America
The Crusades (against Muslims in the Holy Land)
Crusade against 'pagans' of the Baltic (1193)
Albigensian Crusade against the Cathar 'heretics' of southern
France (1209–1229)
Crusade in Hungary against Mongols and Lithuanians (1314)
Crusade in Italy against political opponents of the papacy (1321)
Crusade in Poland against Mongols and Lithuanians (1325)
Crusade against King Louis IV of Germany (1328)
Crusade against heretics in Bohemia (1340)
Crusade of King Magnus of Sweden against pagans of Finland
(1348)
The corrupt papacy of John XII, Benedict IX and Alexander VI
Simony (the sale of Church benefices)
Child abuse
Sisters of Mercy laundries scandal

The good

Education and healthcare in medieval monasteries
Dr Barnardo's – Thomas Barnardo
The Shaftesbury Society – Lord Shaftesbury
Orphanages – George Müller
The Mothers' Union – Mary Sumner
Cancer care – Douglas Macmillan
Cancer care – Leonard Cheshire
Prison reform – Elizabeth Fry
Social housing – Octavia Hill
Sunday and church schools – Robert Raikes
The Ragged Schools Union – William Wilberforce
Braille system for the blind – Louis Braille

World Literacy – Frank Lauback
The Salvation Army – William Booth
The hospice movement – Dame Cicely Saunders
Microfinance for poor countries – D. Bussau
Save the Children – Eglantyne Jebb
Education of the deaf – Thomas Gallaudet
Social work in the US – Jane Addams
Foster care – Charles Loring Brace
Alcoholics Anonymous – Bill Wilson and Bob Smith
Tearfund
The YMCA – George Draper
The Leprosy Mission – Wellesley Bailey
Amnesty International – Peter Benenson
Oxfam
Shelter – Revd Bruce Kenrick
CAFOD
WaterAid
Christian Aid
The Children's Society – Edward Rudolf
Christians against Poverty – John Kirkby
Livability
Habitat for Humanity – Millard Fuller

Further reading

I found the following websites invaluable in preparing this study book. You may wish to explore them and others further as you prepare for or work through this course.

William Wilberforce

http://en.wikipedia.org/wiki/William_Wilberforce
http://www.bbc.co.uk/history/0/
http://abolition.e2bn.org/people_24.htmly/historic_figures/wil berforce_william.shtml
http://www.spartacus.schoolnet.co.uk/REwilberforce.htm

Lord Shaftesbury

http://en.wikipedia.org/wiki/Anthony_Ashley-Cooper,_7th_Earl_of_Shaftesbury
http://www.spartacus.schoolnet.co.uk/IRashley.htm
http://www.historylearningsite.co.uk/children_industrial_revol ution.htm

Florence Nightingale

http://en.wikipedia.org/wiki/Florence_Nightingale
http://www.bbc.co.uk/history/historic_figures/nightingale_flor ence.shtml
http://www.spartacus.schoolnet.co.uk/REnightingale.htm
http://www.biography.com/people/florence-nightingale-9423539?page=4

Martin Luther King

http://en.wikipedia.org/wiki/Martin_Luther_King,_Jr.
http://www.bbc.co.uk/history/people/martin_luther_king.shtml
http://www.spartacus.schoolnet.co.uk/USAkingML.htm
http://www.nobelprize.org/nobel_prizes/peace/laureates/1964/ king-bio.html

http://www.let.rug.nl/usa/documents/1951-/martin-luther-kings-i-have-a-dream-speech-august-28-1963.php
http://www.apartheidmuseum.org/truth-and-reconciliation-commission-trc

Nelson Mandela

http://www.sol.com.au/kor/19_03.htm
http://www.christiantoday.com/article/nelson.mandela.and.his.faith/34956.htm
http://www.christiantoday.com/article/nelson.mandela.and.his.faith/34956.htm
http://www.telegraph.co.uk/news/worldnews/nelson-mandela/10140763/Nelson-Mandela-seized-the-opportunity-of-the-Rugby-World-Cup-1995.html

For useful quotations, the following sites are but some of many:

www.brainyquote.com
http://www.goodreads.com
http://forusa.org/blogs/for/peace-quotes-around-world/10231